B

what i *love* about you

♥

what i *love* about you

kate marshall *and* david marshall

broadway books   new york

for:

_____

from:

_____

date:

_____

*L*ife's greatest happiness is
to be convinced we are loved.

Victor Hugo, *Les Misérables*, 1862

i want you to know that you are loved and that
knowing you has made my life richer. I hope
this journal gives you a fraction of the happiness
you've given me. Thanks for being part of my life.

_____

_____

_____

what i *love* about you

♥

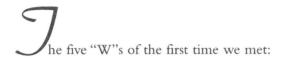

The five "W"s of the first time we met:

*W*hen it was

_____

_____

*W*here we were

_____

_____

*W*ho was there

_____

_____

*W*hy we were there

_____

_____

*W*hat we were doing

_____

_____

*I*f we'd met in a comic strip, the thought bubble over my head would've said:

*W*e clicked because we were:

___ Bread & Butter (complementary)

_____

_____

___ Two Peas in a Pod (kindred spirits)

_____

_____

___ Sweet & Sour (opposites attract)

_____

_____

*A*s I got to know you, I became even more interested because:

_____

_____

_____

_____

I tried to impress you by:

_____

_____

_____

_____

*A*s our romance progressed, we were like:

___ A slow-simmering soup that just got better and better

___ The perfect jeans—soft and comfy right from the start

___ A symphony, with all the parts in perfect harmony

___ A roller coaster with ups and downs, but always a thrill

___ Oil and vinegar, at first clashing but then discovering we were really good together

___ A couple of alley cats in heat

I first knew I loved you when:

_____

_____

_____

_____

_____

_____

_____

_____

_____

_____

Of the many happy times together, this one stands out in my mind:

_____

_____

_____

_____

Do you remember this romantic time together?

_____

_____

_____

_____

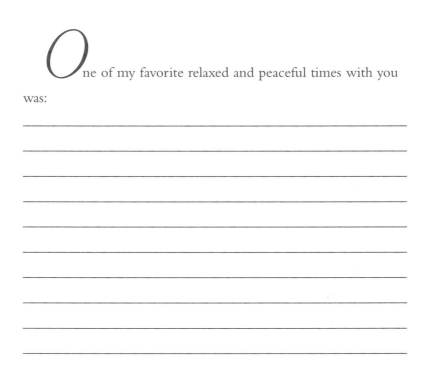

*O*ne of my favorite relaxed and peaceful times with you was:

_____

_____

_____

_____

_____

_____

_____

_____

_____

_____

I'll never forget how funny it was when:

_____

_____

_____

_____

I still can't believe that we:

_____

_____

_____

_____

$\mathcal{W}$e were lucky when:

_____

_____

_____

_____

$\mathcal{I}$ felt especially close to you when:

_____

_____

_____

_____

I missed you when:

_____

_____

_____

_____

*D*o you remember when we shared this sad or difficult time?

_____

_____

_____

_____

$\mathcal{M}$y favorite picture of you is:

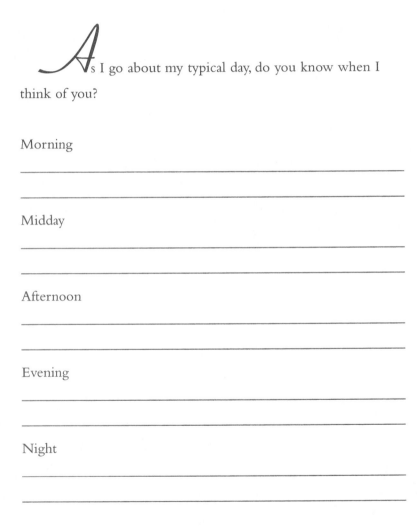

*A*s I go about my typical day, do you know when I think of you?

Morning

_____

_____

Midday

_____

_____

Afternoon

_____

_____

Evening

_____

_____

Night

_____

_____

I love doing this together:

_____

_____

_____

*M*y favorite place to hang out with you is:

_____

_____

_____

I adore this little daily ritual or habit we have:

_____

_____

_____

I love these things we do on:

Friday or Saturday nights

_____

_____

Saturdays or Sundays

_____

_____

Weekdays

_____

_____

Weeknights

_____

_____

Rainy days

_____

_____

Beautiful days

_____

_____

Summer days

_____

_____

First thing in the morning

_____

_____

Last thing at night

_____

_____

*S*o many sensations remind me of you:

Sounds

_____

_____

Tastes

_____

_____

Smells

_____

_____

Touches

_____

_____

Sights

_____

_____

*M*y favorite holiday to spend with you is _____
because:

_____

_____

_____

_____

*W*e celebrate "us" each year on these dates:

_____

_____

_____

_____

*I*f I were making a time capsule from our time together now to open in twenty years, I'd enclose:

_____

_____

_____

_____

_____

_____

_____

_____

_____

_____

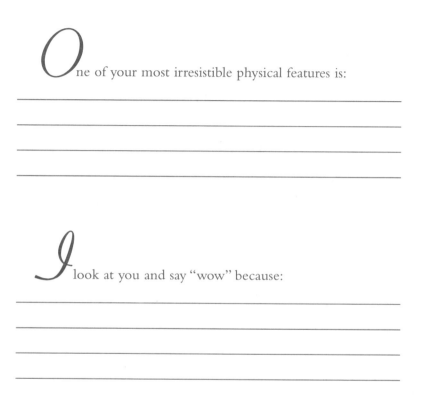

*O*ne of your most irresistible physical features is:

_____

_____

_____

_____

I look at you and say "wow" because:

_____

_____

_____

_____

*W*hen you walk into a room:

_____

_____

_____

_____

I love this facial expression you make:

_____

_____

_____

_____

	When You Wear:	*You Look:*
Piece of Clothing	_____	_____
	_____	_____
Whole Outfit	_____	_____
	_____	_____
Color	_____	_____
	_____	_____
Hairstyle	_____	_____
	_____	_____
Other	_____	_____
	_____	_____
	_____	_____

One of your most impressive physical talents is:

_____

_____

_____

_____

And when you do that it makes me:

_____

_____

_____

_____

*Y*ou'd be the perfect double for:

TV or Movie Star

_____

_____

Other Famous Person

_____

_____

Super Hero

_____

_____

Friend or Family Member

_____

_____

$\mathcal{T}$he ten words that describe you best are:

__ Affectionate	__ Imaginative	__ Spiritual
__ Ambitious	__ Lively	__ Spontaneous
__ Brave	__ Optimistic	__ Steady
__ Careful	__ Passionate	__ Strong
__ Confident	__ Patient	__ Stylish
__ Considerate	__ Playful	__ Thrifty
__ Creative	__ Protective	__ Tolerant
__ Flexible	__ Responsible	__ Tough
__ Friendly	__ Sensitive	__ Wild
__ Funny	__ Sensual	__ Willing
__ Generous	__ Serious	__ Wise
__ Gentle	__ Silly	__ Other
__ Honest	__ Smart	_____

*Y*ou really showed who you are when:

_____

_____

_____

*O*ne of my favorite parts of your personality is:

_____

_____

_____

*A*nd that side of you comes out when:

_____

_____

_____

$\mathcal{T}$o me your heart and soul look like:

*S*omething quirky about you that I find adorable:

_____

_____

_____

*Y*our laugh sounds like:

_____

_____

_____

*Y*ou seem happiest when you:

_____

_____

_____

One of my favorite stories about you is:

_____

_____

_____

_____

_____

_____

_____

_____

_____

_____

*H*ere's something I'd never change about you:

_____

_____

*Y*ou are:

Sweet as

_____

Strong as

_____

Smart as

_____

Beautiful as

_____

Brave as

_____

29

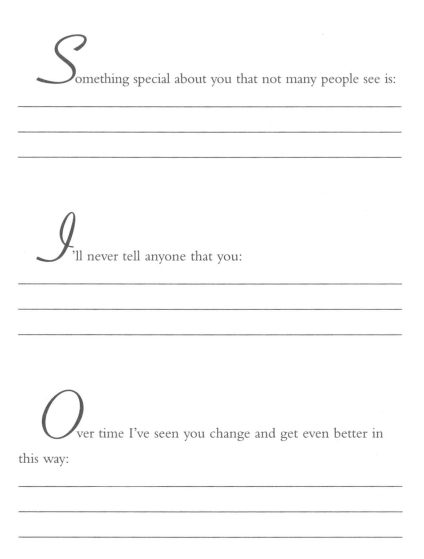

*S*omething special about you that not many people see is:

_____

_____

_____

I'll never tell anyone that you:

_____

_____

_____

*O*ver time I've seen you change and get even better in this way:

_____

_____

_____

*T*he five talents of yours that I'm most addicted to:

__ Cooking

__ Baking

__ Barbecuing

__ Gardening

__ Telling Jokes

__ Massaging

__ Kissing

__ Home Decorating

__ Cleaning or Organizing

__ Planning Vacations

__ Never Getting Lost

__ Managing Money

__ Listening

__ Advising

__ Comforting

__ Making Friends

__ Hosting Parties

__ Selecting Wine

__ Singing

__ Playing Music

__ Creating Art

__ Programming the VCR

__ Handyman Skills

__ Computer Know-How

__ Other

_____

_____

$\mathcal{I}$'m impressed by how much you know about:

_____

_____

_____

_____

$\mathcal{I}$ never tire of hearing you talk about:

_____

_____

_____

_____

*M*y favorite joke or story you tell is:

_____

_____

_____

_____

_____

_____

_____

_____

_____

I get a kick out of watching you:

_____

_____

_____

_____

I respect how you overcame:

_____

_____

_____

_____

$\mathcal{I}$ was proud to know you when:

_____

_____

_____

I hereby award _____

the honor of

Best _____,

for achievement

in the field

of _____.

Dear Sir/Madam,

I am pleased to enthusiastically recommend _____
for the position of _____. In the _____ years
that I have known this person, I have observed an uncanny
ability to _____. I have never known a better
_____ in my life.

If you are looking for the best person to _____
_____, look no further. This candidate is
_____ and _____. It has truly been
my pleasure to _____.

Sincerely,

_____

*W*hen I'm feeling playful, I call you:

_____

_____

_____

*A*nd sometimes you call me:

_____

_____

_____

*S*ometimes I think you should have been named:

_____

_____

_____

$\mathcal{D}$o you know what you can spell with the letters in your name?

_____

_____

_____

_____

_____

_____

_____

_____

_____

_____

_____

_____

_____

_____

_____

_____

_____

When I write your name vertically on this page, I can use each letter to start a new word that describes you (e.g., D is for dashing, donut-devouring dreamer; A is for arrestingly attractive artist . . .):

Your letter: *Stands for:*

_____   _____

_____   _____

_____   _____

_____   _____

_____   _____

_____   _____

_____   _____

_____   _____

_____   _____

*I*f you were a landscape painting, you'd be:

__ Mountains (powerful and steadfast)

__ Grasslands (easy, rolling fields with honest, wide-open skies)

__ Ocean (sparkling on the surface, deep and expansive below)

__ Woodlands (protective, gentle, and tranquil)

__ Rain forest (lush, fertile, and bursting with life)

__ Snowscape (bright yet soft and subtle, quiet, and magical)

__ Desert (hot, hot, hot)

__ Other

_____

*I*f you were a soup, you'd be:

___ Chicken Noodle (everybody loves it)

___ Tomato (smooth, classic good taste)

___ Organic Vegetable (wholesome and healthy)

___ Seafood Gumbo (hot and spicy)

___ Beef Stew (hearty and satisfying)

___ Other

_____

$\mathcal{M}$ore "If you were a ___, you'd be a ___":

Fruit or Vegetable

_____

Wine or Beer

_____

Cereal or Breakfast Food

_____

Animal

_____

Flower or Tree

_____

Something Found in a Kitchen

_____

Body Part

_____

Car

_____

Electronic Device

_____

Country

_____

Magazine

_____

Restaurant

_____

Toy or Game

_____

*I*f I could introduce you to anyone in the world—past, present, or future—it'd be:

_____

_____

_____

_____

*I*f little girls are made of sugar and spice and everything nice, and little boys are made of snips and snails and puppy dogs' tails, you are made of:

_____

_____

_____

_____

*I*f I knew I was going to be stranded on a desert island with you, I'd pack:

_____

_____

_____

_____

*I*f we were stuck in an elevator for the weekend together, we'd:

_____

_____

_____

_____

A good title for your memoirs would be:

_____

_____

_____

_____

R eviewers and readers would say:

_____

_____

_____

_____

*I*f I lost you, I'd post this Missing Person flier:

LOST

Physical Description:

_____

Last Seen Wearing:

_____

Place Last Seen:

_____

Reward:

A is for

_____

_____

_____

M is for

_____

_____

_____

O is for

_____

_____

_____

R is for

_____

_____

_____

E is for

_____

_____

_____

*L*oving you has made me:

_____

_____

_____

_____

*S*ince being with you I've stopped:

_____

_____

_____

_____

$\mathcal{S}$eeing you makes my insides go:

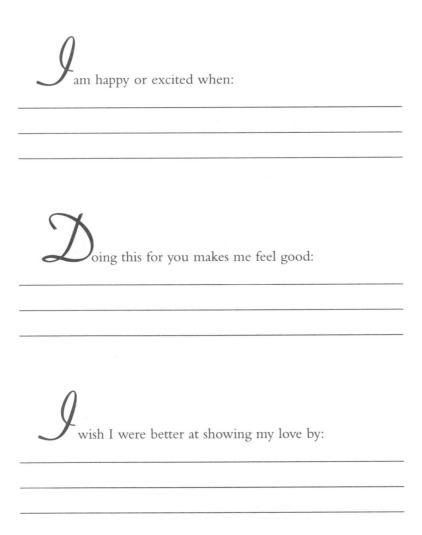

I am happy or excited when:

_____

_____

_____

D oing this for you makes me feel good:

_____

_____

_____

I wish I were better at showing my love by:

_____

_____

_____

$\mathcal{M}$y feelings for you are best expressed by this:

Color

_____

_____

Song

_____

_____

Household Object

_____

_____

Animal Sound

_____

_____

Weather Pattern

_____

_____

*I*f I hadn't already met you, the Personal Ad I'd write to find you would say:

I am

_____

_____

I am seeking

_____

_____

For

_____

_____

If this sounds like you

_____

_____

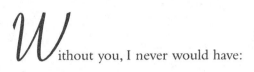

*W*ithout you, I never would have:

Met these very special people

_____

_____

_____

_____

Had this opportunity or experience

_____

_____

_____

_____

*T*hank you for showing me how to:

_____

_____

_____

_____

*Y*ou taught me this about getting the most out of life:

_____

_____

_____

_____

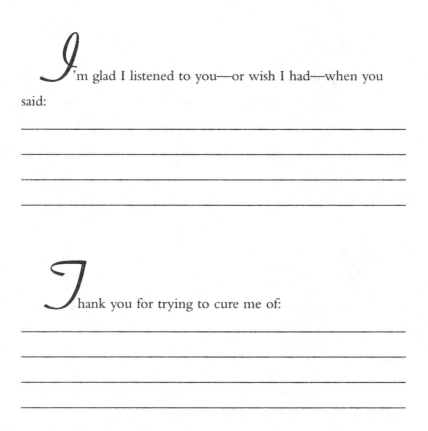

I'm glad I listened to you—or wish I had—when you said:

_____

_____

_____

_____

*T*hank you for trying to cure me of:

_____

_____

_____

_____

𝒴ou taught me this about myself:

_____

_____

_____

_____

𝒴ou inspired me to:

_____

_____

_____

_____

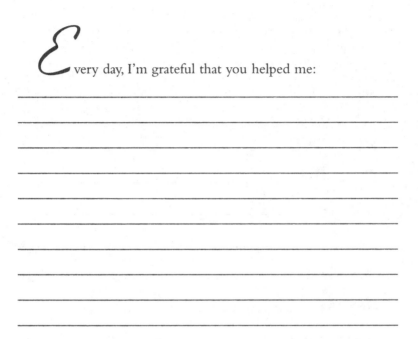

*E*very day, I'm grateful that you helped me:

_____

_____

_____

_____

_____

_____

_____

_____

_____

I'm glad you've been with me to share some big life events:

___ First Kiss _____

___ First Time _____

___ Graduation _____

___ New Job _____

___ New Car _____

___ New Home _____

___ Stage Performance _____

___ Music Concert _____

___ Sporting Event _____

___ Wedding _____

___ Major Birthday _____

___ New Pet _____

___ New Baby _____

___ Promotion _____

___ Financial Win _____

___ Financial Loss _____

___ Other Big Loss _____

___ 15 Minutes of Fame _____

___ Grandchild _____

___ Major Injury/Illness _____

___ Lucky Win _____

___ Surprise Party _____

___ Empty Nest _____

___ Retirement _____

___ Other _____

$\mathcal{Y}$ou changed my feelings or opinions about:

Person I know

_____

Famous person

_____

Love

_____

Social issue

_____

Politics or Politician

_____

My work

_____

$\mathcal{D}$o you know what the best gift you've ever given me was?

_____

_____

_____

_____

$\mathcal{O}$ne of the nicest things you've ever done was:

_____

_____

_____

_____

*T*hese are a few little pleasures you introduced me to:

Delicious things to eat or drink

_____

_____

_____

_____

Entertaining things to watch or read

_____

_____

_____

_____

Places to go, things to do

_____

_____

_____

_____

Practical things to do or use

_____

_____

_____

_____

Things that feel so good

_____

_____

_____

_____

Other things that make me happy

_____

_____

_____

_____

$\mathcal{Y}$ou are the only one I know who will:

_____

_____

_____

_____

$\mathcal{I}$ appreciate how hard it was for you to give this up for me:

_____

_____

_____

_____

I love that you:

Never

_____

_____

_____

Sometimes

_____

_____

_____

Always

_____

_____

_____

$\mathcal{I}$ love when you:

_____

_____

_____

_____

$\mathcal{I}$ was really glad you were with me when:

_____

_____

_____

_____

$\mathcal{Y}$ou made me feel appreciated when you:

_____

_____

_____

_____

$\mathcal{I}$t felt wonderful when you paid me this compliment:

_____

_____

_____

_____

$\mathcal{Y}$ou've helped our relationship work by:

_____

_____

_____

_____

$\mathcal{T}$his was a time I didn't feel loveable but you loved me anyway:

_____

_____

_____

_____

$\mathcal{W}$ith you I feel safe enough to:

_____

_____

_____

_____

_____

_____

_____

_____

_____

$\mathcal{M}$y life *without* you:

$\mathcal{M}$y life *with* you:

*T*hese people or animals love being with you:

_____

_____

_____

_____

*D*o you know this person looks up to you?

_____

_____

_____

_____

*P*eople who work with you are lucky because:

_____

_____

_____

_____

*Y*ou are (or would be) a wonderful parent because:

_____

_____

_____

_____

$\mathcal{I}$f hearts could speak, I imagine the hearts of these people saying to you:

Your Mother

_____

_____

Father

_____

_____

Daughter

_____

_____

Son

_____

_____

Your Sister/Brother

_____

_____

Friend

_____

_____

Boss or Teacher

_____

_____

Coworker

_____

_____

Other

_____

_____

$\mathcal{I}$ love seeing you with your friends because:

_____

_____

_____

$\mathcal{I}$ like that with *my* friends and family you:

_____

_____

_____

$\mathcal{D}$ o you know what I admire about how you are with *your* family?

_____

_____

_____

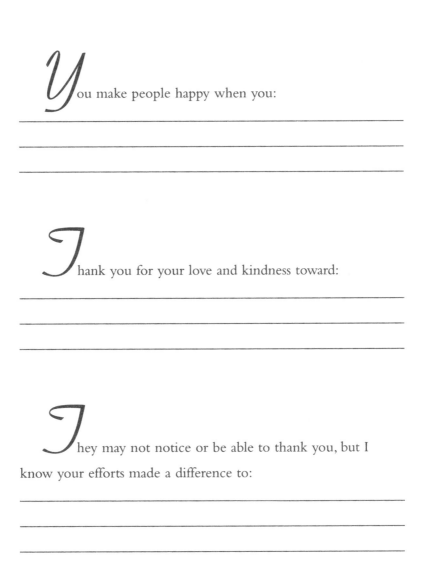

$\mathcal{Y}$ou make people happy when you:

_____

_____

_____

$\mathcal{T}$hank you for your love and kindness toward:

_____

_____

_____

$\mathcal{T}$hey may not notice or be able to thank you, but I
know your efforts made a difference to:

_____

_____

_____

*Y*ou helped make this happen:

_____

_____

_____

_____

I respect your contributions to:

_____

_____

_____

_____

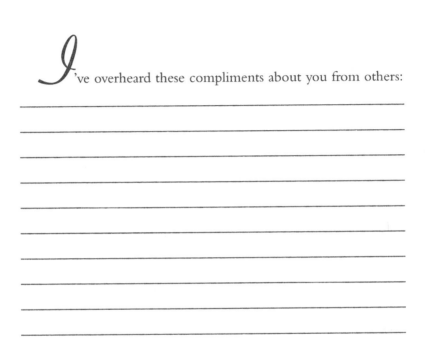

I've overheard these compliments about you from others:

_____

_____

_____

_____

_____

_____

_____

_____

_____

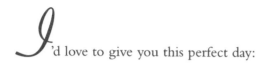

I'd love to give you this perfect day:

Morning

_____

_____

_____

Midday

_____

_____

_____

Afternoon

_____

_____

_____

Evening

_____

_____

_____

$\mathcal{N}$ext Valentine's Day I want to spoil you by:

_____

_____

_____

_____

$\mathcal{F}$ast-forwarding ____ years, this is a wonderful scene I expect to see you in:

_____

_____

_____

_____

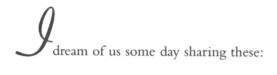

I dream of us some day sharing these:

Places

_____
_____
_____

Adventures

_____
_____
_____

People

_____
_____
_____

Celebrations

_____
_____
_____

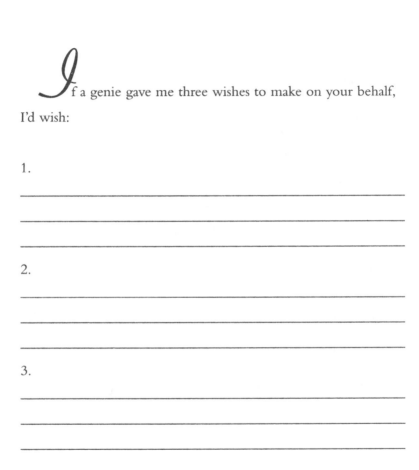

*I*f a genie gave me three wishes to make on your behalf, I'd wish:

1.

_____

_____

_____

2.

_____

_____

_____

3.

_____

_____

_____

*A*ccording to the paper today, your horoscope is:

_____

_____

_____

_____

*B*ut according to my own divine insight, your horoscope
should be:

_____

_____

_____

_____

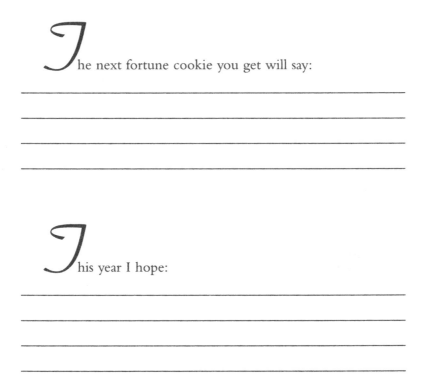

$\mathcal{T}$he next fortune cookie you get will say:

_____

_____

_____

_____

$\mathcal{T}$his year I hope:

_____

_____

_____

_____

*O*ver the next ___ years, I wish:

_____

_____

_____

_____

*W*hen you're in your golden years, I hope you'll look
back on your life and say:

_____

_____

_____

_____

I promise:

_____

_____

_____

_____

*I*f I knew one of us was going to disappear tomorrow, I'd want to tell you this today:

_____

_____

_____

_____

I still have a keepsake or two from our early times together:

notes

pictures

drawings

guest writers

ticket stubs

news clippings

poems

etc.

from the authors

We created this journal to celebrate love. Whether you give *What I Love About You* to someone you treasure or receive it from someone who treasures you, you are lucky. May you always love, be loved, and be thankful.

Kate and David Marshall,
happily married since 1984
www.marshallbooks.net
P.O. Box 6846
Moraga, California 94570-6846